ABOVE: *This splendid AEC Mammoth Major Mk III was completed just in time for the Coronation in 1953. The chassis was available with either one or both rear axles driven, and with the option of an articulated rear bogie. Air pressure brakes were fitted to the Mk III although they only operated on three axles — the second steering axle being unbraked.*

COVER: *A Ford model AA truck built in 1931 and used for most of its working life by a builder. It was in a derelict condition when bought by its present owner and has been completely restored.*

OLD LORRIES

John Woodhams

Shire Publications Ltd

CONTENTS

 First published 1985. Shire Album 138. ISBN 0 85263 732 2.

Set in 9 point Times roman and printed in Great Britain by C. I. Thomas & Sons (Haverfordwest) Ltd, Press Buildings, Merlins Bridge, Haverfordwest, Dyfed.

ACKNOWLEDGEMENTS

I would like to thank all who have helped with information and photographs in the preparation of this book, and in particular Mr D. Thomas, Mr G. C. Sparshatt and Mr J. A. Golding. Photographs on the following pages are acknowledged to: the Boots Company Ltd, 8 (upper), 9 (upper), 21 (upper); ERF Trucks Ltd, 23 (upper), 30, 31; Esso Petroleum Company Ltd, 2, 3, 6, 11 (upper), 15 (lower); Ford Motor Company Ltd, 8 (lower), 15 (upper), 24 (upper), 25 (lower); L. Gardner and Sons Ltd, 26 (lower); J. A. Golding, 32; Harrods Ltd, 7; Hestair Dennis Ltd, 14; Lacre Ltd, 5; London Brick Company Ltd, 22, 25 (upper); Marks and Spencer plc, 21 (lower); Sparshatts of Hampshire Ltd, 1, 10, 11 (lower), 12, 17, 18, 19, 26 (upper), 29 (upper); Taylor Woodrow Ltd, 4; Vauxhall Motors Ltd, 20, 23 (lower). The cover photograph and those on pages 9 (lower), 13, 16, 24 (lower), 27, 28 and 29 (lower) are by the author.

This 1910 Commer was used by the Anglo-American Oil Company (as Esso Petroleum was then known) for kerosine delivery. Commer fitted a unique gearbox, called the Linley gearbox after its designer, which featured a series of dog clutches to engage gears. Changing gear could cause some unusual clicking noises which led the manufacturer to use the slogan 'dogs that bite with a click'. The change speed lever can be seen mounted on the steering column just below the steering wheel. The crescent-shaped plate below the registration number plate reads 'Commercial Cars Luton'.

Thornycroft built petrol-driven lorries from 1902, rated at 2 tons capacity. This vehicle was used from 1904 by the Anglo-American Oil Company to carry lamp oil in the London area. The wooden-spoked wheels show the evolution of the motor lorry from the horse-drawn wagon. The chain drive to the rear axle can also be clearly seen.

THE EARLY YEARS

From 14th November 1896 it was no longer necessary for a man to walk in front of a mechanically propelled vehicle carrying a red flag, and engineers were encouraged to develop the motor vehicle. During the 1890s the motor industry was developing apace in France and Germany, but Britain was lagging behind. A German engineer, Nicolaus Otto, had developed a four-stroke internal combustion engine, made possible by the earlier invention by Lenoir of the sparking plug, and Gottlieb Daimler, who had built his first four-wheeled motorcar in 1886, started to produce petrol-driven lorries in 1896. These early Daimler lorries had many features of the horse-drawn vehicle, including steel-tyred wooden-spoked wheels with wooden brake blocks.

In France Serpollet, Bouton and Count de Dion were among the early pioneers. A partnership between Count de Dion and Bouton prospered, and they soon offered a range of petrol vans, in addition to steam wagons and tramcars. Many of these early commercials were exported to Britain.

Several of the early British manufacturers initially built steam wagons but saw that the future lay with the motor lorry. Thornycroft built its first petrol-engined lorries in 1902, and the Lancashire Steam Motor Company introduced petrol vehicles and changed its name to Leyland Motors Ltd. Early Leyland models included the X type 3½ tonner, introduced in 1907, fitted with a 35 horsepower (26 kW) engine, and the S type 2 tonner available from 1909. Daimler sent large quantities of bus and lorry chassis parts to England, where they were assembled in Shropshire by G. F. Milnes, a tram

Pierce-Arrow was originally an American car manufacturer and entered the commercial vehicle market in 1911. The vehicles shown in this spectacular display are 5 tonners based on the original 1911 design. They would have been imported as chassis only and then bodied locally — hence the detail differences in cab design.

builder, and marketed as Milnes-Daimlers. In 1903 Milnes-Daimler offered a 2½ ton lorry for £550, whilst a two-cylinder Arrol Johnston 12 horsepower (9 kW) 2 tonner cost only £300. A heavier 20 horsepower (15 kW) lorry with a 6 ton payload was already being built by Germain. Straker-Squire imported the Bussing chassis, although most of these were bodied as buses.

The majority of petrol lorries of this time were normal control (that is, the driver sat behind the front-mounted engine), although a number of forward-control lorries (that is, with the driver sitting beside the engine over the front axle) were built by the Lancashire Steam Motor Company in 1905 and then more notably by Karrier of Huddersfield. Very little protection was provided for the driver as most vehicles had no form of cab roof whatever, although sometimes a canvas cover was used in inclement weather. At this stage, vehicles were chain-driven although Dennis introduced worm drive in 1904. Dennis was originally a bicycle maker but became a major lorry producer, latterly specialising in fire appliances and municipal vehicles.

Petrol and steam engines were not the only forms of power being promoted. Broom and Wade offered an unsuccessful single-cylinder paraffin lorry, and experiments were made with battery-electric lorries and vans. Because of battery limitations, these were suitable only as short-range delivery vehicles. Harrods, the Knightsbridge store, was an early user of battery electrics. Initially they used Walker vans but later assembled their own vehicles from proprietary components. Most of the pioneers of electric vehicles were American, although Mercedes and Austro-Daimler built electric vans with an unusual hub motor. These were sold in Britain under the name Cedes.

Scottish builders were Albion (which used the slogan 'Sure as the sunrise') and Halley, which first offered petrol-driven lorries in 1905. Lacre (derived from Long Acre Car Company) produced a variety of trucks and vans including, from 1909, the O type 2½ tonner, of which many were sold to the Belgian army. After the First World War Lacre specialised in road sweepers and other municipal vehicles, building over four hundred three or

ABOVE: *The first Lacre vans were built in 1904, rated at 25 hundredweight (1270 kg) carrying capacity, and with 16 horsepower (11.9 kW) Lacre engines. Many were supplied to London stores as delivery vehicles. In 1905 one Lacre van travelled laden from London to Swansea non-stop in eighteen hours — a considerable achievement for the time.*

BELOW: *Lacre built a range of commercial vehicle chassis before specialising in street cleansing equipment, probably the most famous model being the O which was originally introduced in 1909 as a 2 tonner. The bed of this lorry has been fitted with longitudinal seats. Although fitted with twin tyres at the rear, both tyres would be fitted to one wide wheel rim.*

four wheel L type road sweepers. Wolseley and Alldays and Onions, both Birmingham based, built lorries in addition to motor cars and agricultural machinery but had left the field by 1918.

A new magazine, *The Commercial Motor,* was launched in 1905, and in 1907 the first Commercial Vehicle Show was held at Olympia, London.

An interesting alternative to the conventional clutch and gearbox drive was the 'petrol electric', in which the petrol engine drove a dynamo which in turn powered an electric motor to drive the vehicle. Daimler and Wolseley experimented unsuccessfully with the principle about 1906, but in 1908 Tilling-Stevens converted a Hallford chassis, which led to the production of petrol-electric lorries and buses. The advantages of the system were easier driving and smooth starting, but it suffered cost and weight disadvantages and lost favour as the conventional type of vehicle improved. The Commer chassis built by Commercial Cars of Luton incorporated a pre-selector gearbox, while Dougill and Forrest used friction drives to alleviate the gear-changing problem.

Many early lorries had been fitted with two-cylinder petrol engines, but de Dion Bouton had used a single-cylinder power unit for their light commercials. Gradually more vehicles, such as Milnes-Daimlers, were fitted with four-cylinder engines, and Halley was the first to fit a six-cylinder unit to a heavy lorry in 1919. Early engines were very slow revving by today's standards, with a maximum speed of about 1300 revolutions per minute. Several types of valve gear were tried, including the 'Knight' sleeve-valve engine used by Daimler, which had two concentric sleeves with valve ports for each cylinder. Most engine builders favoured the four-stroke cycle with poppet valves, and the cylinder blocks of four-cylinder engines were often cast in pairs, with separate crankcase castings. Many early chassis frames were of flitch plate construction, that is with the main longitudinal members consisting of timber (usually ash), faced on each side with steel plates, and Daimler continued to use these until the mid 1920s. Early steel frames used rolled steel sections, which led to very heavy chassis. Gradually pressed steel frames took over because they could be built cheaply in quantity and had a high strength to weight ratio.

From 1909 a tax of 3d a gallon was imposed on petrol fuel, making the heavier motor lorry less competitive with the steam wagon.

Pickfords ran their first motor lorry in 1908, and Carter Paterson, a large parcel carrier, bought their first petrol van, a Daimler, in 1897.

A 4 ton Liberty chassis bought as government surplus by Esso in 1920. It continued to serve in the Nottingham area until 1932. Note that as a fire precaution the exhaust pipe does not pass below the tank.

Harrods of Knightsbridge used a fleet of Walker 10 hundredweight (508 kg) battery-electric delivery vehicles. This van was delivered in May 1915 and was still in service in 1938. During the 1920s it was modified for use as a special bread delivery van and fitted with a windscreen and cab doors.

MILITARY AND CIVILIAN USES 1914-29

When war was declared the government owned relatively few lorries, but almost immediately fleets of privately owned vehicles (such as those of Carter Paterson) were commandeered. The War Office had operated a subsidy scheme whereby owners of specified vehicles were paid an initial lump sum and an annual premium for maintenance, subject to the War Office being able to purchase the vehicles when required.

Albion, Dennis, Karrier and Leyland were manufacturers which built many subsidy lorries. Leyland produced over five thousand 3 ton trucks for the Royal Flying Corps, known as 'RAF Leylands'. Austin built large numbers of trucks and from 1913 to 1916 produced a distinctive 2/3 tonner with 'coal scuttle' type bonnet and two separate propeller shafts passing through the chassis side members to each rear wheel. Many of these were sent to Russia, but a large number, which had been built for a cancelled export order, were still being sold on the home market as late as 1922. AEC built over ten thousand of their Y type 45 horsepower (34 kW) 3/4 ton trucks, fitted with Tyler engines for the War Office, and Commer supplied over three thousand 3 ton RC model trucks, fitted with their pre-selector gearbox.

One firm to commence building lorries at the outbreak of war was Guy Motors of Wolverhampton, which introduced 30 hundredweight (1524 kg) and 2 ton lorries. They were fitted with White and Poppe engines and featured an additional overdrive gear. Other commercial vehicle builders were forced to alter their production to wartime goods, as government vehicle orders went mainly to the bigger firms. At this time American manufacturers such as Locomobile (later Riker), White, Liberty and FWD established themselves in the British market.

LEFT: *This 32 horsepower (23.8 kW) Albion 3 tonner was a wartime vehicle, bought in 1921 by Boots and used for long distance work. It was fitted with a windscreen and cab doors.*

BELOW: *The Ford model TT Tonner was a larger version of the famous model T and was designed for a 1 ton payload. It was available from 1917. It is said that when starting from cold proved difficult it was sometimes necessary to jack up the rear wheels. This overcame the resistance of the transmission and epicyclic gearbox and allowed the engine to be turned more freely.*

During the war some operators converted their lorries to run on coal gas because of the uncertainty over petrol supplies. The first experiments with this fuel had been made in 1908-9. Vehicles were fitted with enormous inflatable bags containing the gas, but in the 1920s gas-making equipment which could be carried on board was developed.

When the war ended large numbers of government vehicles were available for disposal. Leyland purchased a former aircraft factory at Kingston-upon-Thames and repurchased as many of its War Office products as it could trace, some of which it had to transport back from the continent. Over three thousand lorries were overhauled and sold with a two-year guarantee. Many surplus American lorries were also on the second-hand market and Peerless reconditioned their products at Slough.

ABOVE: *This pair of Thornycroft 40 horsepower (29.8 kW) J types were supplied new to Boots. Although originally a subsidy design, production of a modified J continued in the early 1920s. They have pressed steel disc wheels with solid tyres.*

BELOW: *The Thornycroft 32 horsepower (23.8 kW) engine used in the J type from 1913 is a typical example of the First World War period. The cylinder blocks are cast in pairs, separately from the crankcase, and the valve springs and linkages are not totally enclosed. A simple updraught carburettor is fitted.*

Scammell exhibited their prototype articulated tanker in 1921. The first lorry had a rectangular tank, but this was superseded by a round tank with separate frame, which in turn progressed to the frameless tank shown here. An early customer was Shell-Mex, but from 1925 a blower unit could be fitted to allow the discharge of heavy viscous liquids.

Major improvements were made in vehicle design in the 1920s. Pneumatic tyres were available from about 1912, although they did not become universal until the late 1920s. Solid tyres were not finally outlawed on new vehicles until 1933, although they were penalised by a speed limit of 12 miles (19 km) per hour in 1928. Many lorries retained their original solid tyres on the rear wheels but were fitted with pneumatic tyres at the front. The pneumatic tyre had been patented by John Dunlop. Its advantages were that it allowed higher road speeds, was less prone to overheating and was less damaging to road surfaces. The Italian-built Fiat 15TER lorry was fitted with pneumatic tyres from its introduction in 1913. Over four hundred of these 30 hundredweight (1524 kg) trucks were supplied to the British forces.

Cab roofs were being fitted by the end of the war period and then windscreens and side windows were introduced. The right-hand gear change of early lorries was replaced by a central control and self starters were another improvement. Oil and acetylene lamps were replaced with electric lighting, and bulb horns were replaced by klaxons and electric horns. Brakes, which had often operated only on the transmission shaft or on the rear wheels, progressed to all-wheel systems. The hand throttle control became secondary to a foot pedal, which was commonly situated centrally between the clutch and brake pedals.

At the 1921 Olympia show Scammell exhibited a 2000 gallon (9092 litre) articulated tanker. The first articulated lorry had been built in 1898, but Scammell was the first firm to produce them in significant numbers and developed an automatic coupling which enabled easy attachment of semi-trailers. The coupling consisted of two ramps attached to the rear of the tractor chassis, to take a pair of flanged wheels on the retractable undercarriage of the trailer. Two coupling hooks on the tractor securely held the trailer undercarriage, and the whole combination was locked by a cab control. Advantages of the system were the high payloads possible and that a trailer could be left for loading and unloading while the tractor was used with another trailer. Scammell is a name associated with heavier vehicles and in 1929 built a 100

ABOVE: *A contrast in size with the Scammell tanker. This delightful little tanker is believed to be a Morris 1 ton of around 1924 and clearly shows artillery style wheels.*

BELOW: *Many lorries originally built with solid tyres were converted to run on pneumatics, particularly after the speed limit for such vehicles was raised in 1928 to 20 mph (32 km/h). Often only the front wheels were converted, but this AEC 2½ tonner has been completely modified. The electric headlamps are also probably a later modification.*

ABOVE: *Although W & G made some goods vehicles in the 1920s, a passenger chassis was used for this horse transporter. A number of coachbuilders specialised in livestock transporters, notably Vincents of Reading, who built their first body in 1928. Horse transporters were often finished to a very high standard.*

BELOW: *Vulcan introduced the VSD model 2 tonner in 1920, with a choice of solid or pneumatic tyres. By this time a worm-driven rear axle was commonplace, particularly on lighter vehicles, although the footbrake acted only on the transmission shaft. The cab of this lorry has a home-made appearance.*

This little Bean was built as a car in 1926. It was converted to a truck about five years later and used by a firm of engineers in Billingshurst, West Sussex, until 1960. A winch handle can be seen to the rear of the cab door.

ton tractor unit, which had a fuel consumption of one gallon per mile. A small cabin was located at the rear end of the trailer for the steersman, who communicated with the driver by telephone. The machine, which was described as the 'world's largest lorry', had a maximum speed of 6 miles (10 km) per hour. The power unit was originally a Scammell four-cylinder petrol engine rated at 80 horsepower (60 kW), although this was replaced by a Gardner diesel in the 1930s. Until this vehicle appeared the very heavy haulage contracts were the province of the steam traction engine.

More European lorries appeared on the British market, including Berliet from France, which had a wide range of vehicles, and Berner from Switzerland. Saurer was another Swiss design, which was built in Britain by Hallford. The United States was building lorries in enormous quantities, using mass-production techniques, and exported large numbers, particularly of the lighter models. Some American manufacturers set up their own factories in Britain, like Ford, which started assembling the Model T at Manchester. The Model T and its larger TT 1 ton sister were built in van and truck form. Powered by a 22.4 horsepower (16.7 kW) engine, they were fitted with a two-speed epicyclic gearbox, transverse leaf suspension and an unusual magneto mounted within the flywheel. The Model T was replaced by the Model A series in 1927. With a three-speed crash gearbox and a more conventional magneto ignition system, the A was rated for a 10-15 hundredweight (508-762 kg) payload, although a larger Model AA was available with a 20-30 hundredweight (1016-1524 kg) capacity. Ford introduced a new range of B and BB models in 1931, and a year later the BB 2 tonner was offered with a 30 horsepower (22 kW) V-8 engine. Ford was an early manufacturer to offer pressed steel factory-built cabs. Many vehicles were purchased as chassis only and then fitted with locally built cabs and bodies. Some larger operators such as Pickfords bodied their own lorries.

British manufacturers enjoyed a growing export market, particularly in the colonies. Leyland was a major exporter, but even the smaller firms were building

The Dennis 30 hundredweight (1524 kg), introduced in 1925, could be bought with solid or pneumatic tyres. A 17.9 horsepower (13.3 kW) White and Poppe engine was used with a three-speed gearbox. This van had a combination of electric headlights and oil sidelights.

lorries for overseas.

Some of the American imports of the war period, notably Jeffrey (later Nash) and FWD (which stood for Four Wheel Drive), featured all-wheel drive. The Jeffrey had four-wheel braking and four-wheel steering as well. The greater off-road abilities of these machines were soon appreciated but Britain did not build its own 4X4 (that is four-wheel vehicle, four-wheel drive) until well into the 1920s. The six-wheeler too was adapted for more rugged use by driving four rear wheels (6X4) or even all six wheels (6X6). Scammell produced the Pioneer 6X6 model in 1929, and many of these were built for heavy haulage overseas and for military purposes. Firms such as County Commercial Cars Ltd specialised in converting standard four-wheel production lorries to six-wheelers to increase their payload. A six-wheel version of the Ford Model AA, known as the Sussex, was available with two driven rear axles.

Thornycroft and Morris Commercial both demonstrated half-track lorries for off-road use. An interesting oddity, which first appeared in 1923, was the Shelvoke and Drewry Freighter. The chassis was fitted with very small wheels and had a very low platform height. The driving position was in some ways more akin to a tramcar and featured tiller steering. The engine was situated transversely behind the driver. Ideal for delivery work, many were bodied as refuse collection vehicles, although a few even received bus bodies.

The American firm Reo (an acronym for Ransom Eli Olds, founder of Oldsmobile) imported the Speedwagon chassis. These lorries were fitted with six-cylinder Gold Crown engines and were capable of a spirited performance. Like many other American builders, Reo fitted wheels with detachable rims rather than the contemporary solid disc wheels.

Between 1926 and 1928 Daimler and AEC joined forces to market their vehicles as ADC (Associated Daimler). From 1928 Daimler concentrated on building buses. Pagefield offered a container lorry from 1922, for refuse collection. The

ABOVE: *The Ford model A replaced the model T in 1927. The A was designed for a 10-15 hundredweight (508-762 kg) payload, whereas the larger AA could carry up to 30 hundredweight (1524 kg). Note the hand-operated tipping gear.*

BELOW: *In 1929 Esso ordered a batch of 1500 gallon (6820 litre) tankers on AEC bus chassis. The low-slung chassis frame, which was swept up over the rear axle, allowed a low centre of gravity for the tank. The vehicle has very little rear overhang. The total unladen weight, and the front and rear axle weights are painted on the chassis side member.*

containers could be winched on and off the chassis. This firm built other specialist vehicles, such as lorry-mounted mobile cranes. Bean Cars Ltd progressed from making cars to trucks, abandoning cars altogether in 1929. Although it offered a range of vehicles up to 4 tons capacity, they did not sell well and production ceased in 1932. The first Gilfords appeared in 1925, powered by American Buda engines. Before building its own vehicles, Gilford had reconditioned American-built Garford chassis. Gilfords continued to be available until 1935, and one of its main goods vehicle customers was the Danish Bacon Company.

For the customer requiring a small commercial, Morris introduced in 1924 their 1 ton pick-ups and vans. Trojan produced a series of small vans of 5 to 15 hundredweight (254-762 kg) capacity, fitted with 10 horsepower (7 kW) two-stroke engines coupled to epicyclic gearboxes, and surprisingly, chain drive and solid tyres. It was also quite common around this time for users to cut down cars to serve as smaller goods vehicles.

In 1920 the Roads Act brought about a new system of licensing and registration. From 1921 goods vehicles were subject to taxation based on unladen weight. The fuel tax was abolished at the same time, although it was revived only seven years later.

Over five thousand 'RAF Leylands' were built. This lorry was new in 1917 and was even used as an army transporter in the Second World War.

A variety of Dennis models of the late 1920s and 1930s is shown here. Nearest the camera are 30 hundredweight (1524 kg) trucks which were built from 1925. The fourth vehicle is a forward control version which made its debut in 1930, whilst the next two lorries illustrate the later style radiator. Finally there is a 45 hundredweight (2286 kg), introduced in 1933, and with a set-back front axle.

THE ARRIVAL OF THE DIESEL ENGINE

Dr Rudolph Diesel had made a compression ignition engine in the 1890s, in conjunction with MAN, a German engine manufacturer. Problems with fuel injection prevented its successful application to a road vehicle for many years, but MAN exhibited an oil engine (as it came to be known) suitable for truck use at the 1924 Berlin Motor Show. Many were convinced that its use would improve fuel economy, because of its high thermal efficiency.

The first diesel lorry in Britain was a 5 ton Mercedes-Benz in 1927. Few were sold because of high import duty and high initial cost. Some Swiss-built diesel Saurers followed before the first British-built diesel truck appeared in 1929. This was developed by Kerr Stuart, a railway locomotive builder, but it was not successful, partly because the 11 litre engine weighed well over a ton, and the project was abandoned. L. Gardner and Sons, of Patricroft, were at this time building the L2 diesel range, which had originally been designed for marine use. They had experimented with semi-diesels and evolved a successful mechanical fuel injection system. (Early diesels used a blast of air to force fuel into the engine.) Firms like Thornycroft, Walker and Company (who built Pagefield lorries) and Guy successfully fitted L2 engines to their chassis. Thornycroft used a six-cylinder engine in a lorry of 15½ tons gross weight, whilst Walkers also experimented with Petter two-stroke engines. Gardner introduced the LW series engines for vehicle use in August 1931, while Leyland and AEC developed their own oil engines. The diesel soon proved to be more economical; whereas a petrol lorry might average 8 miles (13 km) per gallon, a diesel of similar size would return 15-16 miles (24-26 km) per gallon. In addition, diesel fuel was cheaper, although in 1934 a short-lived tax discouraged its use. One disadvantage was the greater weight,

ABOVE: *The distinctive 'threepenny bit' radiator was carried by the Dennis Lancet 3½ tonner, built from 1932 until 1935, in both forward and normal control versions. Note the steering box protruding from the cab front.*

BELOW: *In the 1930s Timothy Whites used a fleet of AEC Matadors, often coupled with drawbar trailers, for delivery services to their branches. This lorry had both side and end loading doors. The lower scroll badge on the radiator reads 'Oil Engine'.*

The range of new Leyland models introduced in 1929 were all named after animals, such as Bison, Buffalo and Badger. This specimen was a Bull, which could be ordered with solid tyres, if required, in which case it would be subject to the 12 mile (16 km) per hour speed limit. By 1930 many vehicles were fitted with electric starters although Leyland, for example, still fitted starting handles as standard equipment until the Second World War.

which meant that diesel engines were initially fitted only to heavier lorries. Commer pioneered their use in lighter vehicles, using Perkins and Dorman engines.

Foden, the steam wagon builder, exhibited a 6 ton lorry powered by the Gardner 6L2 engine at the 1931 Commercial Motor Show. A year later Edwin Richard Foden set up a new company to build diesel lorries under the name ERF, and Foden itself decided to concentrate on diesel lorry production. The ERF prototype was a 4 tonner, but in 1935 an eight-wheeler was introduced, followed in 1937 by a six-wheel twin-steer model. All were fitted with Gardner engines. Atkinson converted petrol lorries to diesel using Blackstone engines, before commencing building its own vehicles. In 1934 Foden announced the Fortunner powered by the new Gardner LK series. Both Leyland and AEC produced a range of heavy goods chassis. In 1929 AEC first exhibited the normal control Majestic 6 tonner and the 4 ton forward control Monarch. They produced a rigid eight-wheeler in 1933, the Mammoth Major, which had a gross weight of 22 tons. The Leyland range were given animal names, such as the Bison 4/5 tonner, the Hippo six-wheeler and the aptly named Octopus eight-wheeler. All were available with Leyland diesel engines from 1931. The Cub was a 2/3 ton chassis introduced in 1931, but largely replaced by the Lynx 5 tonner in 1937. A new Light Six 4.7 litre overhead valve engine, made in both petrol and diesel forms, was fitted to the Cubs in 1935. The Beaver 7 ton lorry was a very popular Leyland four-wheeler of the late 1930s, available with a choice of four or six cylinder petrol or diesel engines.

Dennis began to concentrate on lighter 30-45 hundredweight (1524-2286 kg) vehicles, but they too experimented with heavyweights, such as the Octolat 8X8 artillery tractor, which originally had two engines. In 1931 two more American firms opened factories in Britain: Dodge at Kew and Bedford at Luton. Bedford

ABOVE: *The first Bedfords to appear in 1931 were 2 tonners, available with a choice of wheelbase. The shorter 131 inch (3327 mm) version was known as the WHG, whilst the 157 inch (3988 mm) option was the WLG. Both were fitted with the Bedford 26.3 horsepower (19.6 kW) overhead valve petrol engine, with four-speed gearbox and cable brakes. This WHG model has been restored by Vauxhall Motors Ltd.*

BELOW: *In 1936 Bedford introduced a pressed steel cab and modified the wings and radiator grille, as shown by this WS 30 hundredweight (1524 kg) dropside truck.*

ABOVE: *This 1932 Leyland Buffalo 6 tonner was fitted with six-cylinder 38.4 horsepower (28.6 kW) petrol engine. Hydraulic brakes were used with a vacuum servo-assistance. The servo unit can be seen below the cab door.*

BELOW: *This tractor and trailer combination is an unusual hybrid of an articulated vehicle and a drawbar trailer. The rigid coupling on the tractor allows for transfer of weight from the trailer although the trailer has its own front axle, unlike an articulated semi-trailer. The tractor is a 1931 Beardmore Cobra 10 ton chassis with Meadows four-cylinder petrol engine. The vehicle was beautifully restored by Marks and Spencer as part of their centenary celebrations.*

Drawbar trailers are not often seen in Britain today, although more commonplace in mainland Europe. However, in the late 1930s this AEC Matador laden with bricks and complete with trailer would have been a familiar sight. The vertical black object above the fleet number on the cab side houses the semaphore arm electric trafficator.

was part of the giant General Motors concern, and their early lorries closely resembled Chevrolets. The first Bedford 2 ton lorries appeared in April 1931 and could be bought complete for just £240. Larger 3 ton models were available two years later, powered by the same 26.3 horsepower (19.6 kW) petrol engine. The radiator grille was restyled in 1938, when a slightly larger engine, rated at 27.34 horsepower (20.4 kW), was fitted. For several years Scammell offered conversions of Bedford chassis for use as articulated tractor units, but in 1939 a joint Bedford-Scammell tractor unit was marketed. Bedford did not offer a diesel engine option until the 1950s and concentrated on small to medium-sized vehicles.

This Morris Commercial had a very short bonnet and was known as semi-forward control, as the engine extended back into the cab. On such vehicles access to the engine could be very restricted.

ABOVE: *ERF built four, six and eight wheel lorries in the 1930s. This 1935 six-wheeler was followed two years later by a vehicle with twin steering front axles and a single rear axle, designed to reduce tyre scrub. The high standard of lining out is worthy of note.*

BELOW: *The Bedford Scammell articulated tractor unit was introduced early in 1939, consisting of a Bedford chassis with Scammell coupling gear. The 2 ton tractor offered a maximum 6 ton payload, whilst the larger 3 ton unit allowed an 8 ton payload. The maximum legal speed limit is painted on the fuel tank.*

ABOVE: *The Ford 7V was introduced in 1937, to carry either 3 or 5 tons, and with a choice of 24 horsepower (17.9 kW) four-cylinder or 30 horsepower (22.4 kW) V-8 petrol engines. Brakes were cable-operated at the front and rod-operated at the rear.*

BELOW: *The cab interior of this Albion is typical of lorries of the late 1930s and 1940s: a timber frame with steel panelling. Although fully enclosed and glazed, the finish is fairly basic, and with the windscreen well forward of the driving seat the driver had only limited visibility. Many lorries with the engine in the cab were very noisy, especially if diesel-powered.*

In order to stem severe competition, the 1933 Road Traffic Act introduced a new system of control on haulage operators. Three classes of licence were introduced, known as A, B and C licences. The A licence allowed the operator to trade anywhere, whilst the B licence restricted the operating area. The C licence allowed the holder to carry only his own goods. Renewal of licences could be opposed by other operators and the railways.

In 1933 Scammell built a small articulated tractor and trailer combination. Known as the Mechanical Horse, the tractor was a three-wheeler which, with trailer, could achieve a turning circle of only 21 feet (6.4 m). A four-cylinder Scammell petrol engine was used. Karrier also produced similar vehicles, but the concept had been pioneered by Napier. Ultimately the Scammell was the most successful, being much used by railway companies for goods delivery services.

High Speed Gas built a number of prototype gas-propelled lorries from 1933. With on-board gas-making equipment, they were apparently quite successful, although the design did not progress

A 4 ton Leyland Cub delivered to the London Brick Company in 1939. The Cub used either a 29.4 horsepower (21.9 kW) overhead valve petrol engine, known as the Light Six, or a 27.3 horsepower (20.3 kW) diesel unit.

beyond the prototype stage.

The Seddon appeared in 1938. Although designed to carry a 6 ton payload, it was lightly constructed so that it could be operated at 30 miles (48 km) per hour, then the maximum speed limit for goods vehicles of less than 2½ tons unladen weight. It was fitted with a Perkins P6 diesel engine, coupled with a Commer gearbox. Jensen was also interested in very lightweight trucks and built an integral aluminium lorry, with a 6 ton payload.

Another Scammell development was the mobile concrete mixer, in 1931. The 2.3 cubic yard mixer was mounted on a 6 ton chassis and was driven by a power take-off from the vehicle's engine.

Braking was improved by the use of hydraulic systems, often with vacuum servo-assistance to reduce the effort required by the driver.

This Ford 7V was converted for air-raid firefighting. The model was available until 1949, and during the war years many were supplied as tenders to the National Fire Service.

ABOVE: *In the 1930s Dodge built trucks in England, ranging from 30 hundredweight (1524 kg) to 10 tons capacity. This typical example had the shorter of two bonnet lengths available to give a greater platform length. The penalty of the short bonnet was the engine using more cab space. It was common practice at this time for makers to fix their name badges to the bonnet sides.*

BELOW: *An example of the famous Gardner 5LW engine, introduced in 1931 and built until the 1960s. LW range engines were available with from three to eight cylinders. In the 5LW the cylinders were arranged in blocks of three and two, although the crankcase was a single unit. The five-cylinder design was unusual, makers using four or six cylinder engines for vehicle use. The fuel injection equipment can be seen to the side of the three-cylinder block, and the exhauster (to provide the vacuum for braking) is located on the front of the crankcase immediately behind the fan.*

The Morris Commercial C8 Quad 4X4 prototypes were made in the early 1930s. This open truck version with canvas tilt to body and cab was built from 1944 and was preceded by an artillery tractor with a fully enclosed steel body. The circular disc partly obscured by the offside headlight gives the bridge weight limit of the vehicle — in this case 5 tons.

THE SECOND WORLD WAR AND NATIONALISATION

In 1939 few people appreciated the importance of the road transport industry, and consequently it was not long before fuel rationing and the call-up of drivers caused severe difficulties. The government prohibited delivery of new civilian lorries, and makers turned to military vehicles: for example Foden and Dennis built tanks. However, a few civilian trucks were supplied including two Seddons delivered to an Isle of Wight brewery in 1943.

Blackout regulations required masked headlamps, giving only very limited visibility, and the edges of front wings had to be painted white.

Many new vehicles were required for military purposes, and the British forces also used large quantities of American vehicles, supplied under the lease-lend scheme, such as GMC, Chevrolet and Mack.

The Scammell Pioneer was used as a tank transporter and heavy recovery vehicle. The AEC Matador, in 4X4 form, was used as a gun tractor, and a 6X4 version was used by the Royal Air Force as a fuel bowser. Many of these trucks became breakdown vehicles and timber tractors after the war, and some are still in use today. Bedford built over 250,000 vehicles, from the 15 hundredweight (762 kg) MW range to the rugged 4X4 QL, all fitted with the ubiquitous 28 horsepower (21 kW) six-cylinder petrol engine. Austin, which had not made lorries since the early 1920s, introduced the K in 1939. These were known as 'Birmingham Bedfords' because of their similar appearance to Bedfords. The 2 ton K2 chassis was used by the Auxiliary Fire Service, and also as a heavyweight ambulance with a fabric-covered body and open cab sides. The Guy Ant was built as a gun tractor and also as a general service (GS) truck, whilst Morris Commercial built their

ABOVE: *A Canadian Ford 30 hundredweight (1524 kg) Bofors gun tractor. Wartime Canadian Fords and Chevrolets were almost identical, and this cab style was used from 1943. The 30 hundredweight had a thirsty V-8 petrol engine and four-wheel drive. After the war this lorry was bought by a bus company for use as a breakdown tender.*
BELOW: *This 6X6 GMC is fitted with a specialist radio equipment body and an enclosed cab. GMCs built after 1943 had an open cab. These vehicles were amongst those supplied by the USA to the Allied forces under the lease-lend scheme.*

ABOVE: *Thornycroft built the medium-weight Nippy and Sturdy models from 1935. Similar in appearance, the Nippy was a 3 tonner whilst the Sturdy was a 4 tonner. Customers had a choice of Thornycroft petrol or diesel engines or a Meadows petrol engine.*

RIGHT: *Foden tended to concentrate on heavier types of vehicle, including specialised timber tractors. The STG5, first built in 1935, could haul 15 tons by drawbar or 50 tons by winch. The front axle was unsprung and the lorry powered by a five-cylinder Gardner engine.*

Quad, and Leyland the 6X4 Retriever and Hippo 10 tonners. Lorries were required for many specialist purposes such as mobile cranes and generator trucks and even for suitability for transport by air. Several 15 hundredweight (762 kg) lorries and even the 3 ton Bedford QL could be adapted for this role. A popular 5 hundredweight (254 kg) light truck was the Hillman 10 horsepower (7 kW) light utility, adapted from a saloon car design.

When the war ended, large numbers of lorries were sold as government surplus, and several bus companies in southern England bought a batch of 30 hundredweight (1524 kg) Canadian Fords for use as recovery vehicles.

Hauliers were now faced with a new threat — nationalisation. Despite protests, the 1947 Transport Act set up the British Transport Commission, which had powers to acquire haulage businesses and to operate them as British Road Services. The BRS lorries carried the same lion and wheel emblem as British Railways' locomotives. The BRS virtual monopoly was short-lived however, as in 1951 steps were taken to denationalise the industry, although BRS remained in a much reduced form.

In the early 1950s BRS took delivery of large batches of Leyland Octopus 24 tonners and the more unusual Bristol 15 tonners, all eight-wheelers. Bristol mainly built bus chassis, and since they were incorporated within the provisions of the 1947 Act their products were available only to state-owned bus companies and BRS.

A coachbuilt van body by J. H. Jennings was fitted to this ERF model LK44 of 1950. This 5 ton chassis was powered by a Gardner 4LK engine with a five-speed gearbox.

In the post-war period there was a spate of amalgamations and take-overs. Tilling-Stevens and Vulcan were taken over by the Rootes Group, who already owned Commer and Karrier. Crossley, Maudslay and AEC amalgamated to form Associated Commercial Vehicles Ltd. ACV later acquired Thornycroft and Park Royal Vehicles. Leyland bought out Scammell and Albion.

Cab body styles began to change and exposed radiators were gradually replaced by those covered by a fascia panel, and individual makes lost much of their charm and identity. Timber framing for cabs was replaced by steel and lightweight alloys such as Duralumin were used for body panelling.

Sentinel, of steam wagon fame, offered a 7/8 ton diesel lorry with the engine mounted horizontally amidships, and this was available until 1957. Foden demonstrated a two-stroke diesel engine, an idea which was used by Commer for their TS3 three-cylinder engine.

Driving the bigger lorries was still hard work. Sliding mesh, or crash, gearboxes were usual, so that the driver had to use double declutching techniques for all gear changes. Power-assisted steering was not generally available, although braking systems were normally mechanically assisted. The AEC Mammoth Major used air pressure brakes, whilst others still used vacuum or vacuum-assisted hydraulic systems. Experiments were made with exhaust and engine brakes, to provide additional braking power.

THE PRESERVATION MOVEMENT

The commercial vehicle preservation movement first began in the mid 1950s and the Historic Commercial Vehicle Club (now Society) was formed in 1957. The first rally of preserved commercial vehicles was held at the Leyland factory, and in 1962 the first of the annual London to Brighton runs took place. Many interesting lorries have been saved and carefully restored, including some pre-1920 models from Europe.

In addition to the societies listed below there are many regional clubs. Details of these can often be obtained at rallies of old commercial vehicles.

Commercial Vehicle and Road Transport Club, 30 Temple Grove, Bakers Lane, West Hanningfield, Chelmsford, Essex CM2 8LQ.

Historic Commercial Vehicle Society, Iden Grange, Cranbrook Road, Staplehurst, Kent TN12 0EJ.

FURTHER READING

Baldwin, N. *Heavy Goods Vehicles 1919-39.* Almark Publishing, 1976.
Baldwin, N. *Light Vans and Trucks 1919-39.* Almark Publishing, 1977.
Baldwin, N. *Kaleidoscope of Lorries and Vans.* Warne, 1979.
Baldwin, N. *Pictorial History of BRS.* Warne, 1982.
Baldwin, N. *Shelvoke and Drewry.* Warne, 1980.
Baldwin, N. *Vintage Lorry Albums, Numbers 1-3.* Warne.
Bishop, D., and Marshall, P. *Lorries, Trucks and Vans 1897-1927.* Blandford, 1972.
Bishop, D., and Ingram, A. *Lorries, Trucks and Vans Since 1928.* Blandford, 1975.
Cornwell, E. L. *Trucks in Camera: Foden.* Ian Allan, 1981.
Dunbar, C. *The Rise of Road Transport 1919-1939.* Ian Allan, 1981.
Jenkinson, K. A. *Preserved Lorries.* Ian Allan, 1977.
Jenkinson, K. A. *Preserving Commercial Vehicles.* Patrick Stephens, 1982.
Kelly, P. *Road Vehicles of the Great Western Railway.* Oxford Publishing Company.
Kelly, P. *Great Western Road Vehicles Appendix.* Oxford Publishing Company.
Kennett, P. *The Foden Story.* Patrick Stephens, 1978.
Kennett, P. *World Trucks Series, numbers 1-14.* Patrick Stephens, 1978-83.
Klapper, C. F. *British Lorries 1900-1945.* Ian Allan, 1973.
Reed, J. *Trucks in Camera: Bedford.* Ian Allan, 1983.
Reed, J. *Trucks in Camera: Scammell.* Ian Allan, 1982.
Seth Smith, M. *The Long Haul.* Hutchinson Benham, 1975.
Stevens Stratten, S. W. *British Lorries 1945-1983.* Ian Allan, 1983.
Twells, N. *Pictorial Record of LMS Road Vehicles.* Oxford Publishing Company, 1983.
Vanderveen, Bart H. *Kaleidoscope of Bedford and Vauxhall Military Vehicles.* Warne, 1982.
Wright, C. *Trucks in Britain, Volume 1.* Wyvern Publishing, 1983.

MAGAZINES

The Automobile (PPG Publishing Ltd) is a monthly journal which caters for enthusiasts of historic cars and commercial vehicles.

The Vintage Commercial Vehicle Magazine, quarterly, available on subscription from: The Vintage Magazine Company, Taverner House, Axbridge, Somerset BS26 2NN.

Vintage Roadscene (Ian Allan), quarterly, contains articles on historic commercial vehicles.

The Historic Commercial Vehicle Society issues *Historic Commercial,* quarterly.

ERF built this massive six-wheeled tractor unit in 1953; it was one of their first lorries to be fitted with air brakes. The trend towards a flush radiator grille can be seen here.

PLACES TO VISIT

Bass Museum of Brewing History, Horninglow Street, Burton upon Trent, Staffordshire. Telephone: Burton-on-Trent (0283) 45031.
British Commercial Vehicle Museum, King Street, Leyland, Preston, Lancashire PR5 1LE. Telephone: Preston (0772) 451011.
East Anglia Transport Museum, Chapel Road, Carlton Colville, Lowestoft, Suffolk. Telephone: Saxmundham (0728) 2485.
Glasgow Museum of Transport, 25 Albert Drive, Glasgow G41 2PE. Telephone: 041-423 8000.
Museum of Army Transport, Flemingate, Beverley, North Humberside HU17 0NG. Telephone: Hull (0482) 860445.
Museum of British Road Transport, St Agnes Lane, Hales Street, Coventry, West Midlands CV1 1NN. Telephone: Coventry (0203) 25555 extension 2086.
National Motor Museum, John Montagu Building, Beaulieu, Brockenhurst, Hampshire, SO4 7ZN. Telephone: Beaulieu (0590) 612345.
St Austell China Clay Museum, Wheal Martyn Museum, Carthew, St Austell, Cornwall PL26 8XG. Telephone: St Austell (0726) 850362.
Warnham War Museum, Durford Hill, Warnham, Horsham, West Sussex RH12 3RZ. Telephone: Horsham (0403) 65607.

The majority of preserved lorries are privately owned, but many make regular appearances at vintage vehicle rallies during the summer. Road runs are held, such as London to Brighton (first Sunday in May); Trans-Pennine, from Manchester to Harrogate (August); and Bournemouth to Bath (first Sunday in September). Details are available from the Historic Commercial Vehicle Society.

LEFT: *British Road Services inherited a wide range of vehicle types including this Maudslay, photographed in Portsmouth in 1958. The wheel configuration with twin steering front axles and single rear axle was sometimes referred to as a 'Chinese Six'.*
RIGHT: *Seddon entered the commercial vehicle market in 1938 with their 6 tonner, which was designed with an unladen weight of less than 2½ tons and was thus eligible for the 30 mile (48 km) per hour speed limit. Vehicles of over 2½ tons unladen weight were still subject to a 20 mile (32 km) per hour speed limit. The CL model used a Perkins P6 diesel engine.*